a toddlers' travelogue

Little-Known History and Fun Stuff for Parents

Skyye Seawirth

Skyye Seawirth Books
Since Conception in 2012

Mommy
Publisher and Boss
Daddy
Editor and Doodat
Skyye
Writer and Toddler

Published in America by Skyye Seawirth Books
An imprint of Adagio Press

Library of Congress Control Number: 2017948745
ISBN: 978-1-944855-15-4

Cover and interior design: Annie Moon Seawirth
Cover and interior illustrations: Marina K.

P20170915
First Print Edition

Skyye dedicates this book to all you beautiful parents and grown-ups out there, and thanks Grams, Miss Ramirez, Leil Yvette and John Albert for all their uncommon wisdoms

Mommy thanks Skyye for being born

Daddy thanks Ronnie Van Zant and Lynyrd Skynyrd, and the Doobie Brothers for lifelong memories

A Teeny Introduction
of Sorts

"Hi, guys!"
ST PETE BEACH

Hi, all you beautiful parents and grown-ups!

I'm Skyye and I'm from a sleepy little coastal town in Florida. Tourists call it St. Pete Beach, but us locals just call it The Beach, mostly 'cos it's the only beach in the world . . . that us toddlers have been to. Teeny detail.

Soooo, I guess you're wondering why I'm asking you to turn off the widescreen boob tube, set down that glass of chardonnay or can of

Budweiser, stamp out the Virginia Slims or trash the blunt, and stop preparing dinner for six.

Please take a listen to me a bit 'cos, like Ronnie Van Zant used to say when he was belting it out with Lynyrd Skynyrd, "I know a little!"

Methinks he also added, "Baby, I can guess the rest," but you don't need to hear that right now.

Mommy says I need to gain your trust. Daddy nods his head, turns up the music.

"I know a little!"

Lemme just tell you why I'd love your attention. In this book, I'm gonna show a different side to some of the things you learned in school, heard in tv shows and movies and radio, and were taught by all sorts of people in your life.

These are little-known facts that'll hopefully open your eyes a little more and make you go ooo! and wow! If they don't, Daddy says you can come to our house in The Beach and collect your full refund.

Watch out, 'cos Mommy will serve you dinner, and I will make you stay longer so we can have milk and cookies, and you can tell me all about where you come from, who your mommy and daddy are, and other stuff.

Ask my Grams and she'll tell ya everything you know about American history is a big load of poo, that's for sure!

Grams and I often sit on different

sides of the teeter-totter, but I do agree with her on this point.

Grams also likes to say, "If everybody knew the facts, they wouldn't need no useless opinions."

She usually follows that with this doozy: "Stupidity's a gateway drug!"

This is Grams' way of suggesting that all you parents and grown-ups pay attention now or....

Everybody says Grams is an

"acquired taste." In the same breath, they always seem to be repeating her uncommon wisdoms.

After four years on this big beautiful Mother Earth, I thought it was time for me to open up my jukebox of thoughts, ideas and things, and weigh in on stuff, since most other people have an odd way of presenting what they say is the truth, or, as Grams says,

"If everybody knew the facts, they wouldn't need no useless opinions."
"Talkin' a wh
lotta nuthin'
'bout nuthin'."
"Everybo
in this worl
be et up wit
the dumbs!
"Stupidity's a gateway drug!"

"Talkin' a whole lotta nuthin' 'bout nuthin'."

My preschool teacher, a sweet woman of 23 years named Miss Ramirez, begins each class with a tiny prayer and some wisdom things.

One of the wisdoms she likes is this:

"Every day each person can use their inner power to do one little thing to change the world for the better. Personal wealth

"Who can tell us what beautiful treasure lies between our ears?"

lies between your ears. All else is loose change."

My Grams complains to anybody who'll listen: "Everybody in this world be et up with the dumbs!"

That means something like, "consumed to the gills with stupidity."

Grams also likes to remind us all, "There ain't never been a shortage of 12 year olds on this planet."

That means everybody usually acts like a 12 year old, especially when they're mad or scared. Grams does it, too, although I will never tell that to her pretty mug.

Methinks Grams also means that grown-ups just have a really low signal-to-noise ratio, and they allow external noise to drown out the beautiful music in their lives.

Looking around at my little world, even from only three feet above sea level, I see what Grams means, and at the same time, like Miss Ramirez tells us, I also see a whole lotta beautiful parents and grown-ups who just need a little patient nurturing, that's all.

What they know now does not make them dummies, as Grams likes to call 'em.

Would you want someone calling you a dummy?

Me, neither!

But I do admit that we get lazy at times and need a little talkin'-to.

Miss Ramirez says amen to that, 'cos if we slack off, then our once-bright future becomes a shadow that holds us in place while the rest of the world keeps on scootin' along.

Lemme tell you more about why I decided to write this little book, something special we can all enjoy and be proud to be a part of.

It's mostly 'cos society these days isn't allowing a kid to be a kid, and blaming it on all you parents.

It's not parents' fault. You're just doing what you were taught by your parents and what society whispers to you when you're not lookin'.

These days, no one has time to read a manual on how to be a parent. If there are any manuals, they're written by someone with a PhD or MD, so you wouldn't understand 'em anyway.

Grams says parenting is like "swimming in a milkshake: first few gulps taste like heaven, then you drown."

Please don't think I'm whoopin' up on parents or professionals.

Sorry, but I can't speak for Grams on this one.

I do have an issue with companies and institutions that take advantage of all of us and treat us like dumb sheep and cattle so they can make a buck!

Take a listen to this one:

College football programs are

now recruiting kids as young as nine years old! That's only five years older than me!

They're barely outta diapers and some heartless program wants to convince them to sign their life away for money, prestige and maybe a chance to play in the national championship 10 years down the line.

That's the big theme of the 21st century: kids being trained by people other than their parents

to become grown-ups waaay too soon. And it's hurting everybody!

When I go to preschool and see my peers not laughing and playing like me, makes me sad 'cos they're acting like grown-ups. And there's no one to play with!

Some parents who work three jobs have their 10-year-old girls and boys take care of the other kids and babies.

When does a child get to be just a child!?

It's *deja vu*: the Dark Ages have invaded all over again and this time they're not going away. There's not even a Renaissance in sight.

The big irony is when society and its big businesses try in vain to replicate all the great qualities and memories of childhood: joie de vivre, everything is fun, life is a grand game, all-day play, boundless curiosity, telling the truth, stuff like that.

Most of it doesn't even work
on today's grown-ups 'cos they
missed out on a lot of childhood
and so they don't understand
some of these fun things.
You'd think these big businesses
would know a teeny detail like
that.
Methinks they shoulda hired me
as a business consultant.

To get a leg up on the neighbors,
parents start teaching their

children *in utero*, only seconds after conception.

Couldn't they have waited a few minutes to cool down from all the rubbin' going on? Some people are in a rush, I guess.

I'm not complaining here, 'cos my parents actually did this with me ... for reasons they felt were important. Mommy is a veterinarian and works with disabled and homeless kittens. Daddy's an electrical engineer and musician who loves to play '70s rock with his band buddies at beach bars around Tampa Bay.

Together, Mommy and Daddy make a whole new entity that's more powerful than either of them, as Daddy puts it. It was that special entity, the both of them, that decided to teach me all kinds things early on.

But, in general, when society takes away a kid's childhood, that child loses out on a lot. Sure, they grow up fast and jump right into the job market so they can pay taxes, and interest on credit cards and loans, but they also don't learn some very important things you can only learn when you're a kid.

Like how to be curious and explore, ask questions about everything, have fun, belly-laugh, play in the mud, trust people, and play well with others.

It's important to remember

that kids are natural sponges
of all kinds of information and
experiences.

We kids are born biologists and naturalists, physicists and chemists, geologists and anthropologists. Some are even accountants, bankers and mortgage lenders right outta the womb.

Childhood is the most intensive learning period in the life of a human. We're not just absorbing massive amounts of data from

outside our bodies, we are learning what it all means and how to put it to good use. It's a scary and exciting time for everybody.

If you stifle all this learning by skipping childhood, a child will never be the same again.

Grams reminded me of something: "You don't know real fear 'til you gotta take care of a little kid who's here one sec, over there the next, then nowhere at all!"

Maybe that's another reason many grown-ups want a child to grow up fast: so parents don't have to worry any more.

These parents sacrifice their child's natural growth and well being to relieve their own anxiety and fear.

Why do some parents start communicating with their children so early?

It was believed in ancient Mayan

and Seminole Indian cultures, for example, that DNA reacts and responds to vibrations emanating from outside the womb: Daddy resting a head on Mommy's tummy and mumbling the classics in 30-second sound bites, 10 times each night for nine months.

What the Mayans and Seminoles forgot to tell us was that all that noise from junk tv and those yukky reality shows finds its way into the womb, as well, throwing into

doubt the quality of education a child actually gets before birth.

Imagine having to listen to reruns of a show featuring a chubby girl who plays with dolls and eats donuts all day! Or hearing fights and battles and wars over real estate, money or who gets the house in the divorce. Or listening to depressing news and false views about people and the world.

When I was safely tucked inside

Mommy, she and Daddy made sure I got the best of everything, from wholesome food to books to music.

Before I was born and just after conception, which was February 26 a few years back, they took me on long walks in parks, way up hiking trails in the mountains, along the seashore in Florida and North Carolina and Virginia.

I was exposed to nature a few minutes after conception, 'cos

Mommy and Daddy went for a long walk on Upham Beach near our home, after they made love to make me.

It was a cool winter night in Florida when all the stars were out to play, the kind of night where you maybe put on a sweater and some socks. Mommy had on a hat and she held Daddy's hand.

Daddy says Mommy was a beautiful clinging vine that plugged into him, gave him

energy, and lit up his world.

After I was born, they would read and sing and talk to me, show me different parts of the world on vacations and excursions, and teach and show me everything they thought was important for my growth.

I was very fortunate to have such caring parents who knew the value of exposing their baby to as much of the world as they could.

I wish all of you coulda been

there with me and sensed everything I did, received the special gifts I got, and been brought into this world with so much experience!

Miss Ramirez says I'm "gifted," because of all the experiences I had long before I was even born, and 'cos Mommy and Daddy spent so much time with me. She also calls me "a magnificent all-American toddler!"

Grams says Miss Ramirez is full

of it, and the reason I'm so smart is 'cos it all came from Grams' side of the clan, especially from Grams.

She says, "I never did any of that for your momma! She was on her own by the time she could walk."

When Mommy hears that, she says, "I was not about to make the same mistakes my mother made, not with Skyye.

"My girl was going to learn about life and people and the world, and learn not just from her own experiences, but precious little gems directly from her Daddy and me."

Grams doesn't think you need to pass on all your experiences to your kin. If ya did, wouldn't leave much room for your own lessons.

Miss Ramirez says my Grams was very "hands-off" and didn't like to meddle.

Personally, and I would never tell Grams I know this, but Grams just had too much else to do in life, with two jobs, a deadbeat husband no one ever talks about, six other kids, and a mortgage to keep up.

She didn't even have a car. Had to take the bus or bum rides everywhere, and she never had time to herself. Not one hobby or pastime to speak of.

All her wisdoms came from living a hard life.

Miss Ramirez thinks we should take more time with our children, which is why I am writing this for you beautiful parents and grown-ups, not that I see you as my children.

Hmmm, now there's an interesting concept: *the child becomes the teacher*. But don't quote me on that, please.

Unfortunately, my idyllic pre-childhood is not like that for every child out there, although I wish otherwise. By the time a typical

HEY, all you grown-ups!
Welcome to my seminar

child is born, they have "read" or been exposed to more than 12,000 stone chiselings, wood carvings, books, YouTube videos, and stuff by philosophers, thinkers and writers like Cicero, Aristotle, Shakespeare, Mao, Marx and Lenin.

Oh, and don't forget all the blogs and articles by modern-day know-it-alls, posers and puppets who disseminate bad stuff on just about everything, thus rendering

us precious children zombies,
slugs and little taxpayers in
training.
   Just 'cos there's a novel way to
preach to everybody doesn't mean
you have to get on your soapbox
and actually preach to everybody.
   My lord, go build a barn or
something!

Some parents watch porn and
wrestling and horror movies all
night. Imagine what that kinda

noise does to a growing baby! The mom of one of my friends took her unborn girl to see *Night of the Living Dead*. Six times.

I wonder how I woulda turned out if I'd been blasted with screams from zombies in that movie, or the sighs and moans, screams and groans from nonstop XXX videos and other forms of "adult entertainment."

Ask me, there's nothing adult about that stuff.

Grams says, "Ain't nuthin' but dirt used to make mud, hon!"

And if you think YouTube is really any better, listen to Miss Ramirez:

"YouTube has entirely too much server space. It's a green light for everyone to upload even the most inane and often hurtful things."

Grams disagrees with Miss Ramirez, 'cos Grams learned how to make moonshine off a YouTube video. Another one taught her how to distribute it across state lines right under the FBI's nose.

Grams was able to retire from it, too, and bought her own minivan and a little house in Pass-a-Grille Beach with a swimming pool.

She swears by YouTube, just so you know.

Mommy and Daddy taught me everything from accounting to physics, plus read me a lot of fun stuff, not that accounting and physics weren't fun.

In one of my physics lessons, Mommy asked me, "SkyyeMyLove, how many molecules of air are displaced when I whisper to you, 'I love you'?"

Is that cool beans or what?

The correct answer to Mommy's question is around 2,936,531,384,401,234,453,579 molecules of air displaced in one "I love you."

I also got miles and miles of memorable reads by great authors

"I love you, Skyye."

who told meaningful stories
that stuck in my little brain and
made me think about more than
silly wizards, potions and baby
dragons.

My parents wanted me to be
a thinker, someone who looks at
stuff and asks questions about it,
tries to see what makes things tick
or go boom.

They wanted to create a
beautiful independent girl who
would be nobody's fool.

Unfortunately, we toddlers are being groomed in every way possible by society to create a race of zombies who do as we're told, never ask questions, follow the kid in front of you, eat all your food, don't talk back, brush your teeth, and wash your hands after going potty.

Funny thing, though: we toddlers are smarter than ever. Lordy lordy, just look at me!

Hey, the IQ scale is currently

being redesigned for this new subspecies of magnificent all-American toddler.

When we reach the age of 12 months and officially become a toddler, we begin a new journey into the land of wonder and make-believe that will follow us all the way to the incinerator or the grave.

Grams says it depends on whether you "wanna be deep fried or just dumped in a hole when your clock runs out."

Hopefully, my travelogues will be an adventurous ride for all you beautiful parents, grown-ups and your kin, and all those eager parents who wanna teach your toddlers a teeny bit about American history and other stuff before the age of three.

I also hope the rest of you won't mind listening to some wisdoms from a precocious four year old.

Look at it this way, all you

beautiful parents and grown-ups: Grams says the beach gospel I share with ya can't be any worse than what you're gettin' from those talkin' heads all around you!

My travelogues are a vehicle to share valuable information about subjects you beautiful parents and grown-ups just don't have time to learn by your lonesome.

Everything in my books is sugar-coated for easy consumption, smooth digestion, passive and

"Relax, it's sugar coated!"

pain-free assimilation, and breezy and effective implementation for the brave and courageous.

From what Miss Ramirez tells me, this information is exactly what you all need from time to time but are too afraid or embarrassed to ask, let alone consult a magnificent all-American toddler like me.

Miss Ramirez also says I have a special obligation to everyone when I share my book. She advised me to capture all the love in my heart and soul, then atomize it and spritz it over everybody.

Miss Ramirez gave me this list of important things to look at when I'm writing. She calls 'em "The Princess Truths":

Analyze a certain area or subject and present the results in a way parents and grown-ups will like.

Educate parents and grown-ups in a subject area they don't have time to study on their own.

Entertain parents and grown-ups with a true story, well told, or a grand fictional one with lotsa wisdoms and funnies.

Encourage parents and grown-ups to share my story with loved ones, friends, colleagues and strangers, and invite them to come along with me on this magnificent journey.

Inspire parents and grown-ups to do something significant in life, because it's the only life you have and you only get to do it once.

Miss Ramirez doesn't believe in reincarnation, so don't even think of trying to put off doing stuff 'til tomorrow or after you die.

She tells us toddlers that parents and grown-ups need special gifts like this book every day.

Humans were designed to love gifts and offerings that inspire them to help others and make the world a better place.

I wanna share Mommy's personal philosophy about life, something

she wrote to me before I was born:
My dearest Skyye,
Life isn't about happiness.
It's about finding purpose and staying busy each day, so you can share it with people you love and care about.
A curious side effect of this is becoming happy.
If you are without purpose and choose only to seek happiness, you will find disappointment. My wish for you is that you find your

passion in life and spread the good cheer!

Love,

Mommy

If I don't get sunburned or washed out to sea, I should be able to write more toddler-tested wisdoms before I grow old and turn five.

Like Grams says, "Stick with me, hon, and I'll learn ya all I know!"

Oh, and for all of you who get distracted easily, Grams says this:

"Eyeballs forward, and your jaws locked in the full upright position!"

Something I want you all to know: I love all you beautiful parents and grown-ups more than turkey cheeseburgers, oxygen and ice tea. Okay, maybe not ice tea!

Let's all have a safe and fun journey!

American History
And Some Other Stuff

This is a travelogue of some little-known facts about American history and other fun stuff only a toddler could dig up and share with you, so please settle in and enjoy this little ride.

If you're worried about having to learn something new, relax: these lessons are teeny and have no bad side effects, like dizziness, drowsiness, blurry vision, headache, bloating, constipation, nausea or diarrhea. The only thing left is having fun and hearing about some stuff you've probably suspected all along!

Grams tells me I should have a disclaimer, so here goes: "Everything I learn ya might be baloney. But I kinda doubt it."

No one actually knows who the first Americans were, 'cos visitors to our shores were always busy erasing any evidence of the previous dudes.

But if you ask the Chinese, they'll say they were the first, even before Caveman Bob and his clan.

The Chinese are probably pretty close, since they own a major division of General Motors, Morgan Stanley, *Forbes* magazine, Motorola mobile stuff, The Waldorf Astoria Hotel, the Chicago Stock Exchange, a major Hollywood movie production company, Smithfield Foods (think: your fave holiday ham!), General

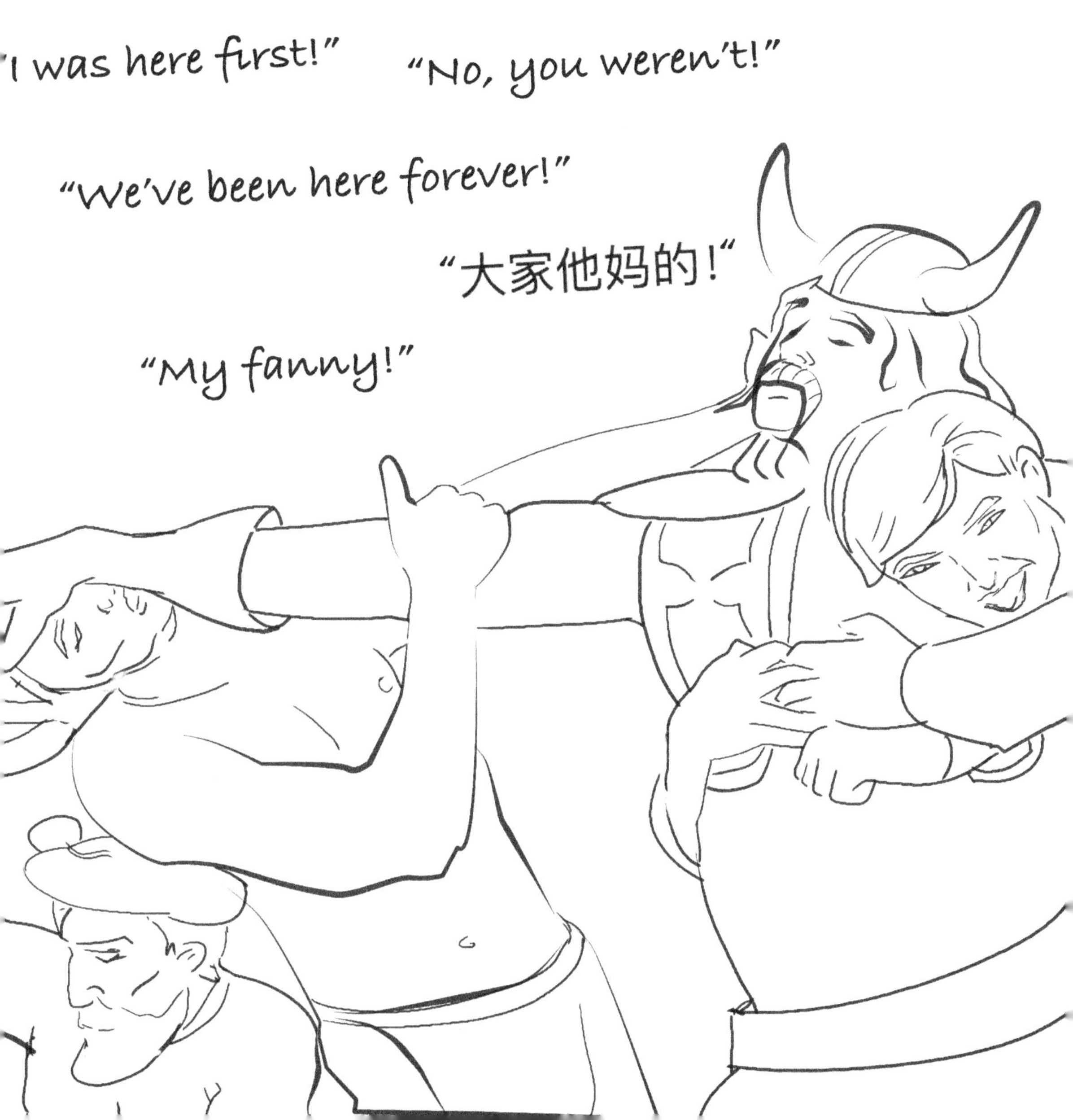
"I was here first!"
"No, you weren't!"
"We've been here forever!"
"大家他妈的！"
"My fanny!"

Electric appliances, Riot Games' *League of Legends*, a major US insurance company, and just about everything else in America.

Ask the French and they"ll say the French (just to be difficult, pro'ly 'cos they're angry that the Chinese already own most of it).

The Scots will say the English (just to be diplomatic so they can quietly secede from Great Britain very very soon).

And the Native Americans will

be pretty doggone honest and tell you the Vikings arrived about the same time they did, because they had a grand feast and barn-burner that lasted 20 spins around the sun, and they shared maps of places they'd visited, Mary Jane, peyote, booze and women.

This explains the curious intermixing of their DNA that produced some very beautiful Viking babies that later populated the urban areas of Scandinavia, fell down the slopes into modern-day Europe, and smartened up all those goth and vandal heathens before they geared up to sack the rest of Europe.

Those Native Americans really got around!

The alternate reality is this, although NASA will probably deny it: a band of extraterrestrials from next door dropped in a few million years back and set up a chemistry lab in the basement,

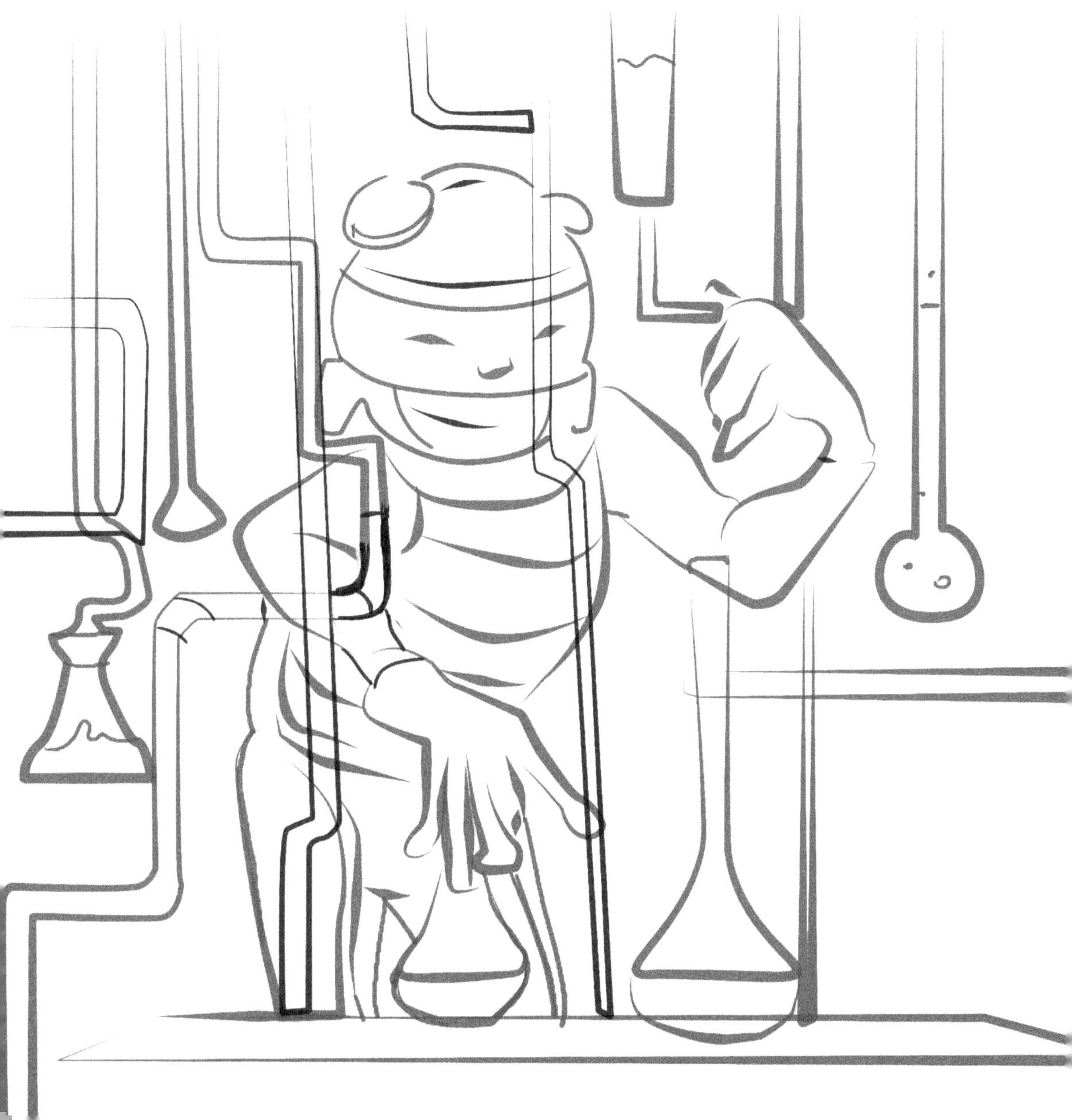

experimented with mixing genes from various monkeys, fish, slugs and ham, and produced the first human, Adam.

He didn't actually have a name, but some ET, upon seeing this iteration, said something like, "Ahh, damn!"

His ET buddies agreed the little guy should be dubbed Adam, after all.

Since the word Adam was not in their lexicon, they invented

it, along with an appropriate definition: "he who plays with and eats own poo."

So, since there exists no accurate history of who the first Americans were, let's just say it was the Native Americans.

After all, they're called *Native* Americans, mostly so they don't rise up again like they did against Custer and hand the US Army its own skinny butt, not that the Native Americans could muster a large-enough army, being scattered over all those forgotten and barren spaces the US government wouldn't dare set their boots in, unless they wanted to go to a casino and party.

If I'd been in charge, I woulda invited the Native Americans over for some milk and cookies, and apologized to 'em for us Americans being so rude and inhospitable all those times.

After all the cookies were gone, I woulda given the Native Americans their land back.

Let's move on!

After the Vikings got bored with all the beauty of America, they discovered they missed their land of frozen sea and ice so they departed, but not before engaging in one final trade: leaving behind a few fair-haired maidens for the Native Americans, and absconding with NA hotties.

Grams reminded me to tell you that NA is not Narcotics Anonymous, by the way, even though one or two of you will argue the point 'til you're blue in the face.

Don't make me hafta do CPR.

Some enterprising, world-traveling conquistadors from Spain shotgunned a few hundred galleons, only a handful of which actually made it, over the Atlantic

to the New World. That would be America.

It was then that the Europeans began to invade our territory.

Now ya know how the Native Americans felt.

When the conquistadors invaded, they brought all forms of pox viruses, syphilis, gonorrhea and their brand of religion, which was all about complete control and everlastin' suffering.

See? That's what I don't get!

How could anyone wanna control a beautiful human being in the first place? To make things worse, they wanna make us suffer, too.

Grams says, "It's faster and easier to be mean and hurtful so you can get your own way. *Kindness* is time and energy most people ain't got."

Yeah, maybe so, Grams, but even if it takes extra energy, I say be kind, decent and respectful the first time, and don't force your views on everyone you meet.

Who wants to be bossed around and told what to do?

For early Americans, the flag of religion, largely rejected by most who felt its wrath, was struck in Maryland, piggy-backed on a few wild viruses, and gradually spread throughout the American colonies, infecting 95% of the population plus a whole lotta people in surrounding counties all the way to California, even though Grams says it was "owned and operated by taco-benders, fajita-flippers and tortilla-stretchers since forever."

Those good people with a strong immunity developed their own forms of spirituality, pissing off some very powerful Men in Black over in Italy.

Rome then countered the protestants with yet more propaganda that eventually worked well enough to bring a lot of 'em into the fold.

The remaining holdouts were forever dubbed anarchists, rabble-rousers, trouble-makers and conspiracy theorists, and were banished to the fringes of society where they eventually invented Rocky Road ice cream, granola and solar panels.

All the Native Americans' prime real estate was quickly slurped up by the invaders, who then had the gall to convert the Natives to their foreign religion.

Rather than convert to a life of pain and suffering, many Native Americans chose homicide and, when that didn't work as planned, they chose the quickest suicide possible to avoid the invaders' religion and all its advertised merits.

This is one of Miss Ramirez' wisdoms: allow people their dignity and they will in turn be kind right back to you.

I've seen this kinda thing on the

playground and in the sandbox, where two kids meet for the first time and one hands the other her toy. The other child says thank you and they play together like old friends.

The flip side is when one kid smacks the other kid over the head with a little hammer and takes his toy. That's when war breaks out and spills over into the neighbor's yard.

Our own Founding Fathers found themselves in that very predicament.

Grams says, "They got all their marching orders from them pizza-slingers and pasta-pullers over in Italy, most of whom had never even set foot on American soil, 'cos they were too preoccupied making all that pizza and pasta and tellin' everybody everywhere what to do all the time!"

The Men in Black from Rome

"We are Founding Fathers, after all. When we hydrate each day, we do it in style!"

wrote all the rules and regulations for Founding Fathers to follow, and ensured the Founders had plenty of distractions: brandy, beer, Mary Jane, opium, women and broadsheets that told 'em how to live, what to think, whom to vote for, and that kinda nonsense.

Word had it, the Men in Black didn't want the Founders to question their masters, let alone rise up against 'em.

Guess what?

It worked famously!
Still does, even though most of you beautiful grownups won't believe it.
Grams says, "Little Skyye knows what she speaks. It's the beach gospel 'round these here parts!"

There were no cherry trees at Mt. Vernon, but there was plenty of alcohol, narcotics and free sex with all kinds of females. Human, too.
The only tree George

Washington ever cut down was a
bushy Mary Jane in his front yard.
Word has it, Washington called it a
cherry tree 'cos, as Grams tells me,
"He was high-high on that damn-
fine Virginia weed, he was!"

The War of 1812 was a light
spanking by the Men in Black,
because Americans evidently
forgot who their masters really
were.
  The Men in Black burned down

the house (the big White one), scorched Washington (the city, not George) and its surrounds, and left an indelible mark not soon forgotten for at least one generation.

Those guys over in Italy reasoned that it would take one or two generations to teach America's children how to obey orders, so they wouldn't ask questions or whine like babies.

How would you like to be

bossed around by people
who don't even live in your
neighborhood? Tellin' you what
you can and can't do, what to eat
and drink, where to live and work.
And on top of it all, making you
pay taxes on just about everything,
including ice cream and cookies!
Just thinkin' about it makes me
mad! Taxin' my cookies. Baloney!

Fast-forward, just so I don't lose
any of you: the Civil War was

designed and planned by the same guys who started tellin' our Founders what to do more than a hundred years before.

They wanted to divide our new nation into at least two major groups, making it easier to control all of us: those who loved turkey, carrots and potatoes, and those who swore by the southern diet of fried chicken, biscuits and gravy, peas and corn.

Heck, I grew up eating both and

I'm pretty healthy!

Those clever dudes in Italy also silenced President Abraham Lincoln 'cos he freed a bunch of beautiful people who were forced to come to America a coupla hundred years earlier.

Who in their right mind would chain another beautiful human being and boss 'em around?

No one.

In their *right* mind.

Grams is fightin'-mad when she

goes, "Where the blazes were all the grown-ups when President Lincoln took a bullet to the peach?"

In 1898, those pesky Spanish conquistadors tried and tried again, but got whooped up on by the US Army in Havana, Cuba.

After a thorough butt-stompin', the Spanish hung up their silver spurs and retired forever from bullyin' all the neighbors, and turned to cultivating some damn-fine vino and Mary Jane (word has it, with virgin buds and seeds they stole from the Native Americans).

I can hear Grams now: "See what happens when ya put your mind to makin' somethin' deee-licious!?"

Since time began, seems that men and boys have always bossed us women and girls around.

I just don't get it!

VOTES
FOR
WOMEN

Without a woman, you can't have kids, unless you're one of those test-tube babies or you fell off the back of some galactic spaceship.

So tell me this, grown-ups: how is it that women didn't get the right to vote until the first part of the 20th century?

And even then, some states still wouldn't let women vote, or their votes were "lost" during the voting process.

Where were all the good men and boys when this nonsense was going on?

My Daddy woulda punched somebody if Mommy couldn't vote. Mommy woulda pulled out her Smith and Wesson and gone a-huntin'.

Still not sure what I woulda done. Heck, I do know, but it gives me gas just to think about it.

And don't even get me started on how minority women and men

were treated.

Nope, don't get me started, grown-ups, 'cos you don't wanna hear what's on my little mind on that subject. Huh-uh.

I try not to get too upset about how women and girls have been treated in history, not just here in America.

We truly are the fairer sex, made to love and not to war. Men have always tried to keep us on a short leash and boss us around.

How's that workin' for ya today,
all you guys who don't respect us
women and girls?
I should write a whole book
on how boys should treat girls.
I'd start with basic wisdoms like
respect, kindness and decency.
Oh, and that one dignity wisdom
Miss Ramirez talks about, too!
They'd make me prez and CTO
(Chief Toddler O'Yeah!).

I realize this might be tough to

swallow, so chase it down with a glass of vino or some ice tea with lotsa sugar: the *Titanic* was steered into an iceberg. Yes, intentionally.

Why?

Don't ask. You won't like the answer.

But hey, the unsinkable Molly Brown survived!

Sadly, Leonardo DiCaprio did not, but his movie made a boatload of cash and made a few gullible grown-ups wonder how the blazes he showed up in *The Revenant* over 100 years later.

This next one outta make you scream and spit!

The Federal Income Tax law was put into effect shortly afterward, although not enough states actually ratified it, 'cos Christmas was going on and everybody was too preoccupied with presents, Mary Jane, beer, booze, opium, peyote and sex.

The Men in Black knew they could do whatever they wanted to all Americans, laws or not, especially when they fooled 'em with all kinds of distractions.

This little tax law is the reason you grown-ups pay so much of your hard-earned dollars to the government, can't always make those mortgage payments, are behind in credit-card bills, have trouble putting food on the table, and can't afford that 55"

LG widescreen, even though it's discounted at WalMart.

Those of you who can afford those things are still mad 'cos you have to pay 39% of your income to the IRS.

Did you know that, in 1945, if you were a top earner, you had to pay 94% of your income to the IRS!? In 1960, it dropped to a measly 91%.

No wonder so many people jumped outta tall buildings and

took up homicide as a hobby.

Please don't shoot me, I'm just the messenger.

When Grams hears about the Income Tax thing, she says, "Never mess with the gods. They ain't got nuthin' but time."

Funny thing, while Grams seems to fear the IRS, she has never paid a penny in income taxes, thanks again to YouTube videos.

WWI brought on all kindsa new

problems: mustard gas and weapons of mass destruction, viruses that only killed young people (that's odd 'cos most natural viruses are equal-opportunity killers), and the first stab at a single world government that would rule everybody everywhere all the time and without a whole lotta laws we Americans could complain about, let alone fight to change.

One good thing: all those

brilliant nurses and doctors (mostly girls, of course!) who marched into battle without a rifle or gun, just to come to the aid of our fallen soldiers.

Go, girls!

Another good thing: fighter ace Eddie Rickenbacker and all the other hunky fighter pilots in their flowing, white silk scarves and those magnificent flying machines!

The League of Nations was a

We Can Do It!

flop, though, which brought on
the next great war that ended
up taking our precious men and
a few women waaaay too soon,
but birthed Rosie the Riveter, War
Bonds, B-17s in the thousands, GI
Joe, General George Patton, the
atomic bombs that sacked some
peeps over in Japan and made
'em stop cuttin' off everyone's
head, an Iron Curtain between the
East and West, and, of course, the
United Nations.

Kinda like the floppy League of Nations but dressed up like a Thanksgiving turkey that was only slightly more edible than the previous iteration, but with all the hazards and poisons of the first one.

Grams says, "Them weenies tryin' to pretty up an old pig with mascara and lipstick. Didn't fool me none!"

While our men and women were

preoccupied with WWII, our precious and valued American farmer was getting sacked at home by someone high up a ladder. They bought up thousands of farms and started to put the American farmer out of business.

Now I'm wondering why Americans let this happen. Huh, huh? Sorry, but I have no funnies or wisdoms for that one.

Makes me cry and cry.

Grams says, over and over,

"Happens all the time: people be et up with the dumbs!"

After WWII sorta turned into world peace, people came home and remembered what they'd been missing for years: SEX.

And they remembered it over and over for days and weeks and months at a time.

In no time, kids like me sprung up like beautiful wildflowers all over the place. In America, we called 'em "baby boomers" and they set the world on fire with all their spending and consumption of just about every known resource, natural and man made, over the entire planet.

Millions of new houses and potties had to be built to accommodate the unchecked growth of these organisms that resembled a cross between monkeys and bacteria.

Don't ask me which bacteria. They're all alike to a four year old.

When America needed to numb the pain from over-consumption of Post Toasties, furniture, refrigerators, and automatic washers and dryers, we started a war with some jungle people in Vietnam we thought we could whoop pretty fast.

If more than 10 years is fast for you, then I guess we accomplished a lot. But we lost a lotta beautiful people in the process.

We also doped up America with

some great heroin and Mary Jane,
sold in our cities and towns.
Just before we got booted outta
Vietnam, there was Richard Nixon,
this president who got impeached
for doing what he did all along:
lied lied lied to everyone, even
to his own face in every mirror he
passed.
He was very impressed with
himself, even though everybody
else thought he was a real boob.

A few years before Nixon was kicked to the curb so he could build his presidential library, some dude named Timothy Leary and his hippy followers found LSD and free love, and the hippies contracted a lotta new STDs that spread across America like, well, sexually transmitted diseases normally do when a whole lotta hippies are doing it while they're hopped up on LSD and Mary Jane and they're going from one anonymous romp to the next.

The innocuous phrases "no strings attached," "no holds barred," "no fine print" and "friends with benefits" were invented then, mostly to confuse and appease parents and grown-ups. Ask me, there's still some confusion.

Grams says grown-ups will find this hard to take, but kids eventually got tired of endless sex. Or just got worn down to the nub.

"Friends with benefits, groovy!"

Didn't those kids ever hear about *moderation*?

Some eventually found college, others religion.

The rest of America found a good job with bennies and a decent retirement package.

Whatever else they found, it brought the extended Summer of Love to a close, and allowed America to wash away the '70s.

It took 10 years and whole lotta soap and water to do it.

Captain America and US Army Airborne Rangers jumped into the tiny Caribbean island of Grenada to rescue some hapless medical students and take down a long runway full of Cuban soldiers with cool gear furnished by the Soviet Union.

Seems we were always tussling with the Cubans and their over-supply of sugar cubes and mojitos.

It goes without saying that we sure enjoyed messin' with that

government over in the Soviet Union every chance we got.

The Soviets were well on their way to total collapse, or at least that's what we were told, but it didn't happen until 1989.

They say Soviet General Secretary Mikhail Gorbachev was the guy behind it all, but things weren't quite what they seemed.

Gorby was famously known for his rather humongous birthmark

on the top of his bald head, a tattoo resembling a large Pacific island.

He was given a big load of American cash and set up with a McMansion in Florida overlooking beautiful Sarasota Bay.

That's what selling dètente for a billion dollars gotcha.

Dètente is a snooty word that means something like, "Chill out, dude. Let's have some beer."

When the communist walls finally
came crumbling down across
Europe and the eastern back-
end, all these Russian oligarchs
absconded with the palace jewels,
including old Soviet nuclear
missiles and bombs, tanks and
airplanes, submarines, and a whole
lotta other prime-A stuff that made
the American spooky spies kinda
nervous, 'cos they lost control of
just about everything they thought
they had control of during the war

that was so cold.

Hundreds of American and Soviet spies were rooted out by traitors on both sides, and there were these secret executions and other grisly offings of some good people.

There was entirely too much on tv for Americans to really notice these shenanigans, since the big media companies were all busy getting bought out by bigger media companies, which had their own colorful agendas, launching thousands of fun and entertaining new movies, tv shows and news programs with the prettiest people on the planet.

They were the ones who broke that teeny story about President Clinton's willy-wonkin' in the Oval Office with Whatshername.

Grams told me to remind you: "He didn't actually inhale any of the other times he smoked Mary

Jane, either."

The Internet was all the rage in the middle and late 1990s, and everyone and her grams were putting up websites, all trying to make a fast buck.

The spooky spies, who sorely missed all the action and excitement of the Cold War, were quick to start companies like Amazon, Facebook, Google and others, 'cos the intelligence dudes saw the time was ripe to sneak into everyone's living room and have a little look-see and poke around some.

The boys at the Spooky Spy Academy dumped millions of dollars in start-up cash into hundreds of new companies, threw them all against the wall and watched to see what would stick.

Lemme give you a hint:

Amazon.

Google.

Facebook.

Oh, and the spooky spies then made it look like these smart college dropouts did all the work.

Some other dudes in the intelligence community were busy spying on Americans to the point the weenies at this other place actually allowed us to know about some of it.

Grams says, "Hon, if that ain't arrogance, it sure looks, smells and

quacks like it!"

Recruiters from the intelligence community actively trolled college and university campuses for smart kids who looked just like sheep, right down to their woolly coats and the familiar BAAAAA!!!

Imagine that: a community of smart sheep.

As an aside: the spooky spies tried to recruit me outta preschool.

I gave 'em a little finger.

But I won't tell you which one.

Mommy tells me to be a lady. Soooo, parent and grown-ups, ya got all this funny stuff going on in society, but you guys don't wanna hear about it!

We toddlers and kids are the ones who inherit all the crapoo people are ignoring.

What a shame, you ask me.

If I were a grown-up, I would take some time to figure out how to make the world a better space for all of us, then invite everyone over for ice tea and crackers to talk the situation over.

What else can a toddler do?

Hush up and play!?

Heck, no! I'm gonna write and tell some stories, shake up the neighborhood, stomp on some feets, kick some booties!

Maybe if I do, then people of all ages will do what Miss Ramirez says: at least take a listen to the wisdoms of a toddler who's seen some stuff, done some deep thinking, and been around the block a few times without getting caught in a drive-by.

Grams says people like to think they know it all, just 'cos they have a good job or went to college or flew up in space.

Baloney!

When Mommy used to tell me to pick up all my toys, I asked, "Why!? Why!? Why!?"

She then took the time to explain all the reasons why I

should pick up after myself, and then it all made sense.

If people just ask basic questions instead of just following all the rules, silly as some are, things in this beautiful world would be a whole lot different.

But ya gotta take an interest in things first, then start askin' lotsa questions.

Grams always tells me:

"If ya want something done right

the first time, do it yourself, or hire a toddler!"

So I went back home and pulled out the book with Grams' wisdoms, stared long and hard at the one about doing it yourself.

While all my little friends were outside playing and learning the art of love and war, I sat down to write this little book, not just for you parents and grown-ups.

It's a gift for everybody in the world, with some wisdoms and things I have learned in my four years on this beautiful place we call Mother Earth.

Grams says, "Heaven sakes, hon, you can learn a lot from a toddler, and you should, too!"

Lemme leave you with a list of all my fave things in life. If ya think on it some, they're all you really need every minute of every day:

Family.

Food.

Fun.
Faith.
Flair.
Fascination.
Fantasy.

Thank you, all you magnificent, all-American parents and grown-ups, for taking the time to go on this fun journey with me!

All my love and wisdoms,

Skyye

www.ingramcontent.com/pod-product-compliance
Lightning Source LLC
Chambersburg PA
CBHW081334080526
44588CB00017B/2623
9781944855154